I0477814

Table of Contents

Introduction

Welcome to "The Ultimate Guide on How to Start a Bookstore Business"! This comprehensive guide is crafted just for you, providing all the information and guidance you need to successfully start and run your very own bookstore. Whether you're a passionate book lover looking to turn your hobby into a profitable venture or an entrepreneur keen on entering the retail industry, this book will be your roadmap to success.

We're going to cover it all from the basics of the bookstore business to the intricacies of managing operations and finances. You'll get a step-by-step guide on choosing the right bookstore model, setting up your store, understanding your target market, and implementing effective marketing and promotional strategies.

Starting a bookstore business is an exciting and rewarding endeavor, but let's be honest, it comes with its challenges. The good news is, with the right knowledge, preparation, and determination, you can build a thriving bookstore that not only caters to the needs and passions of your customers but also generates a sustainable income for you.

Throughout this guide, we'll provide you with practical tips, valuable insights, and real-life examples from successful bookstore owners. Approach each chapter with an open mind, ready to learn, and be willing to adapt the ideas and strategies to fit your unique situation.

So, let's embark on this journey together and explore the fascinating world of the bookstore business. By the end of this book, you'll have all the tools and knowledge you need to turn your dream of owning a bookstore into a reality. Get ready to dive in and make your mark in the literary world!

Chapter 1: Introduction to the Bookstore Business

Starting a bookstore can be an exhilarating and fulfilling venture for book lovers and entrepreneurs alike. In this chapter, we're going to dive into the basics of running a bookstore and give you a solid introduction to help set you on the path to success.

The Allure of Owning a Bookstore

Bookstores have always been beloved cultural hubs, offering a unique gathering place for book enthusiasts. Even with the rise of e-books and online retailers, physical bookstores maintain a special charm. There's something irreplaceable about the cozy ambiance, the comforting smell of books, and the joy of browsing through shelves brimming with various genres. It's an experience that many people still cherish deeply.

The Changing Bookstore Landscape

It's important to understand that the bookstore industry has seen significant changes in recent years. Independent bookstores are experiencing a resurgence, focusing on niche markets and forging strong bonds with their local communities. Specialized bookshops, dedicated to specific genres like children's literature or mystery novels, are also becoming increasingly popular. This evolution in the industry presents both challenges and opportunities for new bookstore owners.

Market Trends and Opportunities

Keeping an eye on market trends is crucial for identifying opportunities and making informed decisions for your bookstore. Despite the stiff competition from online retailers, physical bookstores continue to play a vital role in the industry. Many readers value the social aspects of bookstores, such as the ability to browse in person, attend author events, and receive personalized book recommendations. By tapping into these preferences, you can carve out a niche for your bookstore and attract a loyal customer base.

Overcoming Challenges

Running a successful bookstore isn't without its hurdles. You'll need to navigate potential obstacles like rising rent costs, effective inventory management, and adapting to changing consumer tastes. However, with careful planning and strategic decision-making, these challenges can be managed. It's all about being prepared and staying flexible in the face of change.

The Joys of Starting a Bookstore

Starting a bookstore allows you to follow your passion for books while contributing to the literary community. You get to create a unique space that fosters a love for reading and offers a haven for book lovers. Additionally, owning a bookstore gives you the chance to engage with customers on a personal level, recommend books, and curate a collection that resonates with your target audience.

In the following chapters, we'll explore the various aspects of starting and running a successful bookstore. By understanding the fundamentals and embracing the evolving landscape, you'll be well-prepared to embark on this exciting entrepreneurial journey.

Chapter 2: Assessing Your Passion and Knowledge

Starting any business, including a bookstore, begins with a crucial step: assessing your passion and knowledge. This chapter is dedicated to guiding you through evaluating your love for books and ensuring you have the expertise needed to embark on this exciting journey.

Identifying Your Passion for Books

Passion is the heart and soul of any successful business. Before diving into the world of bookstores, take a moment to identify your passion for books. Ask yourself what draws you to this business. Is it the love for reading? The joy of sharing stories? Or perhaps the desire to connect with others who appreciate literature? Understanding your motivation is key. It will help you sustain the business during challenging times.

Conducting a Self-Assessment

Next, let's conduct a self-assessment to evaluate your knowledge and skills related to books and the bookstore industry. Here are some aspects to consider:

1. **Reading Habits:** Reflect on your reading habits. How diverse is your reading repertoire? Are you familiar with a wide range of genres and authors? A broad knowledge base will benefit your bookstore by allowing you to cater to a wide range of readers.
2. **Literary Knowledge:** Evaluate your understanding of literary genres, current book trends, and classic literature. This knowledge will help you curate a compelling collection of books that appeals to your target market.
3. **Book Industry Experience:** If you have prior experience in the book industry, such as working in a bookstore or publishing company, take note of the skills and insights you've gained. This experience will be invaluable in managing your bookstore effectively.

Continuing Education

If you find any gaps in your knowledge or skills, consider pursuing further education or training. Attend workshops or courses related to bookselling, inventory management, customer service, and marketing. Enhancing your expertise will prepare you to navigate the challenges of running a bookstore with confidence.

Research and Stay Informed

Stay up-to-date with industry trends, new book releases, and changes in reading habits. Engage with book communities, join book clubs, and participate in events or conferences related to the book industry. The more knowledgeable you are, the better equipped you'll be to provide recommendations to your customers and offer a unique experience in your bookstore.

Identifying Your Unique Selling Proposition (USP)

After assessing your passion and knowledge, use this information to identify your Unique Selling Proposition (USP). Your USP is what sets your bookstore apart from competitors and attracts customers. It could be your extensive knowledge in a specific genre, a curated collection of niche books, or a focus on local authors.

Consider these questions to help define your USP:

1. **What makes your bookstore different from others in the area?**
2. **How can you leverage your passion and knowledge to create a unique experience for customers?**
3. **Do you have expertise in a particular genre or a niche market that can be your specialty?**
4. **What kind of atmosphere or ambiance do you want to create in your bookstore that aligns with your passion?**

By thoroughly assessing your passion and knowledge and identifying your unique selling proposition, you are laying a strong foundation for a successful bookstore. Up next, Chapter 3 will delve into understanding your target market and how to tailor your bookstore to meet their needs and preferences.

Let's continue this journey together and build a bookstore that not only thrives but also reflects your love for books and your unique vision.

Chapter 3: Understanding Your Target Market

Running a successful bookstore isn't just about having a great selection of books. It's about knowing who your customers are, what they like, and how they shop. This chapter will delve into how you can get a deep understanding of your target market, which is essential for tailoring your offerings and attracting more customers to your store.

Demographic Information

First things first, let's talk about demographics. You need to gather detailed information about the people living in the area where your bookstore will be. This includes their age, gender, income level, and education level. This demographic data is like a treasure map that will guide you in stocking the right books.

For instance, if your bookstore is in a neighborhood bustling with families and children, you'll want to have a vast selection of children's books, educational materials, and perhaps even some toys. If you're in an area with a lot of young professionals, then focusing on trendy, popular titles across various genres would be more appealing.

Psychographic Information

Next up is psychographic information, which goes beyond demographics to understand the attitudes, interests, and lifestyles of your target market. This helps you figure out what motivates your customers to read and what kind of reading experience they are looking for.

To gather this information, you might consider conducting surveys or focus groups. Even casual conversations with potential customers can be incredibly insightful. Find out what genres, authors, or topics they are passionate about. Are they into fantasy novels, self-help books, or historical biographies? Do they enjoy cozying up with a good mystery or diving into the latest science fiction saga? Understanding these preferences allows you to curate your inventory and create an atmosphere that resonates with your audience.

Behavioral Information

Now, let's dive into behavioral information, which is all about how your customers shop. This includes how often they visit bookstores, whether they prefer physical books, e-books, or audiobooks, and their spending habits. Tracking this behavior can reveal patterns and trends that are crucial for making informed decisions.

For example, you might discover that sales of a particular genre spike during certain holidays. With this insight, you can plan special promotions or events around those times to draw in more customers. Understanding your customers' buying behavior helps optimize your inventory management, pricing strategies, and promotional activities.

Competition Analysis

Don't forget about the competition. Analyzing other bookstores in your area is a key part of understanding your target market. Visit their stores, check out their offerings, pricing, and customer service. Conduct some online research to see how they are engaging with their customers.

This analysis will help you identify gaps in the market and opportunities for differentiation. Maybe there's a genre they're not covering well, or perhaps their customer service could be better. By understanding what your competitors are doing, you can position your bookstore uniquely and offer something they don't.

Conclusion

Understanding your target market is the backbone of a successful bookstore business. By gathering demographic, psychographic, and behavioral information, and analyzing your competition, you can tailor your offerings and marketing strategies to attract and keep your customers. Remember, the key is to continuously monitor and adapt to changes in your target market to stay relevant and meet their evolving needs.

With this knowledge in hand, you're well on your way to creating a bookstore that not only meets the needs of your customers but also stands out in the market. So, let's dive deeper into each aspect and equip you with the tools you need to truly understand your audience and make your bookstore a beloved destination for book lovers.

Chapter 4: Choosing Your Bookstore Model

Choosing the right bookstore model is a critical step for the success of your business. With various models to consider, each offering unique advantages and considerations, it's essential to determine which one aligns best with your goals and target market. In this chapter, we'll explore different bookstore models and help you figure out which one is the best fit for you.

1. Traditional Brick-and-Mortar Bookstore

The traditional brick-and-mortar bookstore is the classic model that most people think of when they hear the word "bookstore." This involves setting up a physical store where customers can browse and purchase books in person. One of the greatest advantages of this model is the ability to interact personally with customers, offering a unique and engaging experience. Additionally, a physical store provides a space for events, book signings, and community engagement, fostering a sense of local culture and connection.

However, it's important to be aware that this model requires a significant investment. You'll need to budget for rent, inventory, staff salaries, and other overhead costs. But, if you're passionate about creating a welcoming space for book lovers in your community, a brick-and-mortar store can be incredibly rewarding.

2. Online Bookstore

With the rise of e-commerce, online bookstores have become a popular option. This model allows you to reach a much broader customer base beyond your local area. Operating an online bookstore typically involves lower overhead costs compared to a physical store. You can sell books through established e-commerce platforms or create your own website.

One challenge with online bookstores is the fierce competition in the digital space. To stand out, you'll need to invest in digital marketing and effective SEO strategies. If you enjoy leveraging technology and reaching customers far and wide, an online bookstore could be the right choice for you.

3. Hybrid Bookstore

A hybrid bookstore combines both a physical store and an online presence. This model offers the best of both worlds: the personal interaction and community engagement of a brick-and-mortar store, along with the broader reach and convenience of online sales. Customers have the flexibility to browse and purchase books in-store or online, which can significantly enhance their shopping experience.

While this model can be more complex to manage, it provides a robust platform for growth and customer satisfaction. If you're willing to handle both physical and digital operations, a hybrid bookstore could be a perfect blend.

4. Specialty or Niche Bookstore

Specialty or niche bookstores focus on specific genres, topics, or interests. Examples include children's bookstores, LGBTQ+ bookstores, or stores specializing in rare or antique books. This model caters to a specific target market, attracting passionate customers who are often willing to pay a premium for specialized knowledge and unique book offerings.

If you have a deep passion and expertise in a particular area, a specialty bookstore allows you to carve out a unique space in the market. Your unique selling proposition (USP) in this model is your specialized knowledge and curated collection, which sets you apart from more general bookstores.

5. Mobile Bookstore

A mobile bookstore is a unique and flexible model that involves operating out of a vehicle or trailer. This approach allows you to take your bookstore to different locations, such as festivals, fairs, and community events. It offers a novel and convenient shopping experience for customers and can help you reach a diverse audience.

Operating a mobile bookstore requires careful logistics and planning, including route scheduling and inventory management. If you love the idea of bringing books to people wherever they are, and enjoy the flexibility and adventure this model offers, a mobile bookstore could be a fantastic option.

6. Secondhand Bookstore

Secondhand bookstores, also known as used bookstores, sell pre-owned books at discounted prices. This model appeals to budget-conscious readers and collectors searching for out-of-print or rare editions. Secondhand bookstores can be standalone businesses or operate as a specialized section within a traditional bookstore.

This model requires a keen eye for quality and value, as well as effective inventory management to ensure a steady flow of interesting books. If you're passionate about giving books a second life and enjoy the thrill of finding rare gems, a secondhand bookstore might be your ideal choice.

Considerations for Choosing Your Bookstore Model

When deciding on your bookstore model, there are several key considerations to keep in mind:

- **Understand Your Target Market:** Consider their preferences, shopping habits, and demand for various book formats (physical, e-books, audiobooks).
- **Analyze Competition:** Identify existing bookstores in your area and their strengths and weaknesses. Look for opportunities to differentiate your offerings.
- **Assess Your Budget:** Evaluate the financial resources required to start and operate each type of bookstore. Consider

the potential return on investment for each model.

- **Identify Your USP:** Determine your unique selling proposition and how it aligns with your chosen bookstore model. This could be based on specialized knowledge, curated collections, or a distinctive customer experience.

Conclusion

Choosing the right bookstore model is a crucial step in starting your business. By considering your goals, target market, and financial resources, you can evaluate the different options and select the one that best aligns with your vision. Remember, your chosen model can evolve over time as your business grows and adapts to market trends.

In the next chapter, we will explore the process of setting up your bookstore. Let's continue this journey and turn your dream into reality!

Chapter 5: Setting Up Your Bookstore

Setting up your bookstore is a thrilling and essential step toward turning your dream into reality. It involves meticulous planning, attention to detail, and a clear vision of the bookstore you want to create. In this chapter, we'll explore the vital steps and considerations involved in setting up your bookstore, ensuring you're well-prepared to open your doors to eager readers.

Location, Location, Location

Choosing the right location for your bookstore is one of the most critical decisions you'll make. The success of your bookstore hinges on its accessibility and visibility to potential customers. Here are some key factors to consider when selecting a location:

- **Demographics**: Research the demographics of the area to ensure there is a demand for your bookstore. Understanding your target market's preferences and habits will help you select a location that caters to their needs. For instance, if your bookstore is in a neighborhood with many families and children, you may want to focus on stocking a wide range of children's books, educational materials, and toys. Conversely, if your target market consists mainly of young professionals, you might focus on trendy and popular titles across various genres.

- **Foot Traffic**: Look for areas with high foot traffic, such as shopping centers, downtown areas, or near educational institutions. High foot traffic increases the chances of attracting potential customers who may stumble upon your bookstore while going about their day.
- **Competition**: Evaluate the proximity of other bookstores in the area. While competition can be healthy, too many nearby bookstores might saturate the market. Consider locating your bookstore in an area with a limited bookstore presence to increase your chances of success.
- **Costs**: Assess the rental costs and overhead expenses associated with the location. It's crucial to find a balance between financial feasibility and the potential profitability of your bookstore.

Once you've chosen a location, ensure it's easily accessible, with ample parking or public transportation options nearby. The exterior of your bookstore should be inviting and reflect the character of your brand.

Store Layout and Design

The layout and design of your bookstore play a significant role in creating an inviting and comfortable atmosphere for customers. Consider the following elements when planning your store layout:

- **Bookshelves and Display Areas**: Strategically position bookshelves and display areas to highlight popular genres and new arrivals. Experiment with different arrangements to create visually appealing displays that capture customers' attention.
- **Book Organization**: Decide on a logical and consistent system for organizing your books. Options include organizing by genre, author, or a combination of both. Clearly labeled sections and signage will make it easier for customers to navigate your bookstore.
- **Reading Areas**: Create cozy reading nooks or designated seating areas where customers can browse through books comfortably. Provide comfortable seating options and ample lighting to enhance the reading experience.
- **Checkout Counter**: Position the checkout counter at a convenient location near the entrance or exit, ensuring it is easily visible to both customers and staff. Make sure to have necessary equipment, such as cash registers or POS systems, in place.

When it comes to the design of your bookstore, align it with your brand and target market. Consider elements like color schemes, lighting, and overall ambiance. A well-designed bookstore will not only attract customers but also encourage them to spend more time browsing and exploring.

Inventory Management

Efficient inventory management is vital for the success of your bookstore. It involves sourcing, storage, and organization of books to meet customer demand. Consider the following strategies for effective inventory management:

- **Curated Selection**: Choose a carefully curated selection of books that aligns with your target market's interests. Focus on quality over quantity, offering a unique and diverse collection that sets your bookstore apart.
- **Ordering and Restocking**: Establish relationships with book distributors or publishers to ensure a steady supply of books. Monitor sales trends and customer feedback to determine which books require restocking and which ones can be phased out.
- **Organization and Categorization**: Organize your books in a logical and easily navigable manner. Use clear labels and signage to help customers find what they are looking for quickly. Regularly update and maintain the organization of your bookshelves.
- **Inventory Tracking**: Implement an inventory management system that allows you to track sales, restocking needs, and overall stock levels. This will help you make informed decisions about ordering, discounts, and promotions.
- **Seasonal and Trend-Based Stocking**: Stay up-to-date with current literary trends

and seasonal demands to offer books that are in high demand. Make sure to stock up on popular titles during holiday seasons and festive periods.

Remember, effective inventory management is a continuous process that requires regular monitoring and adjustment based on customer preferences and market trends.

Technology and Infrastructure

Investing in the right technology and infrastructure is crucial for running a smooth and efficient operation. Consider the following technological aspects when setting up your bookstore:

- **Point of Sale (POS) System**: Implement a reliable POS system that allows for efficient transaction processing, inventory management, and sales tracking. Choose a system that suits the specific needs of your bookstore.
- **Online Presence**: Establish an online presence through a website or e-commerce platform to reach a wider audience. Implement an easy-to-use online bookstore where customers can browse and purchase books.
- **Wi-Fi and Digital Assets**: Offer complimentary Wi-Fi to customers, encouraging them to spend more time in your bookstore. Consider providing access to digital assets such as e-books or audiobooks to cater to customers' varied preferences.

- **Security Systems**: Install security cameras, alarms, and other necessary security measures to protect your bookstore from theft or unauthorized access.

Having the right technology in place will streamline operations, improve the customer experience, and provide valuable insights for business growth.

Conclusion

Setting up your bookstore requires careful consideration of the location, store layout, inventory management, and technology infrastructure. Take the time to plan and execute each step thoughtfully, ensuring that your bookstore provides an inviting and unique experience for customers. With meticulous planning and attention to detail, you'll be well on your way to creating a beloved haven for book lovers.

Chapter 6: Legal and Regulatory Considerations

Starting a bookstore is an exciting venture, but it requires careful attention to legal and regulatory considerations. Overlooking these aspects can lead to costly legal issues and potentially hinder your business's success. In this chapter, we'll walk you through the essential legal and regulatory steps you need to address when starting a bookstore.

1. Business Structure and Registration

One of the first steps in setting up your bookstore is determining the legal structure of your business. You have several options, including sole proprietorship, partnership, limited liability company (LLC), or corporation. Each structure comes with its own benefits and drawbacks. It's crucial to consult with a business attorney or tax professional to determine which structure best fits your specific needs.

Once you've decided on a business structure, you'll need to register your company with the appropriate government agencies. This typically involves obtaining a business license, registering for a tax identification number, and complying with any local or state regulations. Be sure to research the specific requirements for your area and follow the necessary steps to ensure your business is properly registered and legally compliant.

2. Intellectual Property Protection

In the bookstore industry, intellectual property (IP) plays a significant role. It's essential to understand and respect copyright laws when selling and distributing books. This includes obtaining the necessary permissions and licenses for any copyrighted material you plan to use, such as book excerpts or artwork.

Additionally, consider protecting your own intellectual property, such as the name and logo of your bookstore. Registering trademarks can help safeguard your brand and prevent others from infringing upon your rights. Consult with a trademark attorney to understand the process and requirements for trademark registration.

3. Sales Tax and Financial Compliance

As a bookstore owner, you'll need to comply with sales tax regulations. This typically involves obtaining a sales tax permit from your state's tax agency and collecting and remitting sales tax on applicable transactions. Research the specific sales tax requirements for your area and determine the necessary steps to remain compliant.

Maintaining accurate financial records is essential for both legal compliance and effective business management. Consider implementing an accounting system or software to track sales, expenses, and inventory. Keep all financial documents organized, and consult with an accountant or bookkeeper to ensure accurate reporting and tax filings.

4. Employment Laws and Regulations

If you plan to hire employees for your bookstore, it's crucial to familiarize yourself with federal, state, and local employment laws and regulations. This includes understanding minimum wage requirements, overtime regulations, employee classification (such as exempt or non-exempt), and workplace safety standards.

Create an employee handbook that outlines your policies and procedures, including anti-discrimination policies, time-off policies, and expectations for conduct and performance. Consult with an employment law attorney to ensure your employment practices align with legal requirements and to address any specific concerns or questions you may have.

5. Privacy and Data Protection

In today's digital age, privacy and data protection are vital considerations for any business. If you collect and store customer information, such as email addresses or purchase histories, you must comply with applicable privacy laws and regulations. Ensure that you have appropriate measures in place to protect customer data from unauthorized access or breaches.

Implement secure technology systems, train employees on data protection best practices, and regularly review and update your privacy policies. This will help safeguard your customers' information and build trust in your bookstore.

6. Other Legal Considerations

There may be additional legal considerations specific to the bookstore industry or your location. For example, if you plan to sell alcohol or serve food in your bookstore, you'll need to obtain the necessary permits and comply with any regulations related to food and beverage services.

When negotiating a lease for your bookstore location, consult with a commercial lease attorney. Ensure that you understand the terms and conditions of the lease, including rent costs, maintenance responsibilities, and any restrictions on the use of the space.

Conclusion

Addressing legal and regulatory considerations is a crucial step in starting a bookstore business. By understanding and complying with these requirements, you can protect your business, avoid legal issues, and lay a solid foundation for success. Consult with legal professionals and experts in the bookstore industry to ensure you're taking the necessary steps to comply with all applicable laws and regulations.

By taking the time to understand and address these legal aspects, you'll be better prepared to navigate the challenges of starting and running a successful bookstore. Let's continue this journey with confidence and turn your bookstore dream into a thriving reality!

Chapter 7: Marketing and Promotion Strategies

Marketing and promotion are key to driving foot traffic to your bookstore and boosting sales. In this chapter, we'll dive into various marketing techniques and promotional strategies that can help you attract customers and build a loyal base of book lovers.

Identifying Your Target Audience

Before you start any marketing campaign, it's crucial to understand your target audience. Knowing who your customers are allows you to tailor your marketing messages and promotional offers to their specific needs and preferences. Take some time to analyze the demographics and psychographics of your target market. Consider their age, gender, interests, and reading habits. This information will help you develop effective marketing campaigns that resonate with your audience.

Creating a Strong Brand Identity

Building a strong brand identity is essential for establishing your bookstore's reputation and attracting customers. Your brand identity should reflect your bookstore's values, mission, and unique selling proposition (USP). Think about creating a visually appealing logo and consistent branding materials, such as business cards, signage, and website design. Make sure to use your brand's voice and tone consistently across all marketing channels to create a cohesive and recognizable identity.

Online Marketing

In today's digital age, having a strong online presence is vital for any business, including bookstores. Here are some online marketing strategies to consider:

1. **Website**: Develop a user-friendly website that showcases your bookstore's unique offerings, events, and promotions. Include an online catalog where customers can browse and purchase books.
2. **Social Media**: Utilize social media platforms such as Facebook, Instagram, Twitter, and Goodreads to engage with your target audience. Share book recommendations, host virtual events, and run promotional campaigns to generate buzz and increase brand awareness.
3. **Email Marketing**: Build an email subscriber list and send regular newsletters with updates, special offers, and book recommendations. Personalize your emails based on customer preferences and buying history for better engagement.
4. **Content Marketing**: Create valuable and engaging content related to books and reading, such as blog posts, book reviews, or author interviews. This will position your

bookstore as a trusted source of information and attract readers to your website.

Offline Marketing

While online marketing is important, don't forget about traditional offline marketing strategies. Here are some ideas to consider:

1. **Local Partnerships:** Collaborate with local businesses, schools, libraries, and community organizations to host joint events, cross-promotions, or book clubs. This will help you expand your reach and tap into new customer networks.
2. **Print Advertising:** Place advertisements in local newspapers, magazines, or community newsletters to raise awareness about your bookstore and any upcoming events or promotions.
3. **Direct Mail:** Send targeted postcards or flyers to residents in your local area to promote special events, discounts, or new book releases. Ensure your messaging is compelling and includes a clear call-to-action.
4. **Community Engagement:** Participate in local events, book fairs, or literary festivals to connect with book lovers in your community. Sponsor or host author signings, book readings, or writing workshops to deepen engagement with your audience.

Promotional Strategies

In addition to marketing efforts, implementing promotional strategies can help attract customers and boost sales. Here are some ideas to consider:

1. **Loyalty Programs**: Reward loyal customers with a loyalty program that offers discounts, exclusive access to events, or promotional perks. This will incentivize repeat purchases and foster customer loyalty.

2. **Book Clubs**: Create book clubs where customers can gather to discuss and explore literary works in-depth. Offer discounts on club selections or host book club meetings in your store to encourage repeat visits.

3. **Author Events**: Invite local authors or renowned authors in your bookstore's niche to host readings, signings, or Q&A sessions. This will attract book enthusiasts and create a buzz around your store.

4. **Seasonal or Themed Promotions**: Develop special promotions around holidays, such as book gift guides for special occasions or themed book displays for seasonal reading. This will tap into customers' buying interests and encourage impulse purchases.

Evaluating and Measuring Results

Regularly evaluate the effectiveness of your marketing and promotion strategies. Track key metrics such as website traffic, conversion rates, social media engagement, and sales performance. Based on the data and feedback, refine your marketing campaigns to optimize results. Consider conducting customer surveys or gathering feedback to understand your audience's preferences and continuously improve your strategies.

By implementing a mix of online and offline marketing strategies, coupled with creative promotional initiatives, you can effectively reach your target audience, increase brand awareness, and drive foot traffic to your bookstore. Next, in Chapter 8, we will dive into providing exceptional service and experience to ensure customer satisfaction and loyalty.

Chapter 8: Providing Exceptional Service and Experience

Creating an engaging and welcoming atmosphere is essential for providing exceptional service and creating a memorable experience for customers. Your bookstore should feel like a haven for book lovers—a place where they can relax, explore, and indulge in their passion for reading. Let's dive into how you can achieve this.

Creating an Engaging and Welcoming Atmosphere

Store Layout and Design

The layout and design of your bookstore should be thoughtfully planned to optimize customer flow and create a comfortable browsing experience. Think about the spacing between shelves, the lighting, and seating areas. Cozy reading nooks or designated areas where customers can sit and enjoy the books they've selected can make a huge difference. Imagine a customer sinking into a comfortable chair with a book, feeling like they've found their personal reading sanctuary.

Organized and Easy-to-Navigate Shelves

An organized and easy-to-navigate shelving system is crucial for a positive customer experience. Categorize books logically and clearly label each section. Keep your shelves well-stocked and regularly updated to provide customers with a fresh selection. A tidy, well-organized space makes it easy for customers to find what they're looking for and encourages them to explore new genres and titles.

Visual Merchandising

Utilize visual merchandising techniques to capture customers' attention and encourage exploration. Display featured books, new releases, or themed collections prominently. Use attractive book covers, signage, and props to create visually appealing displays that tell a story and entice customers to discover new books. The visual appeal of your bookstore can draw people in and make their visit more enjoyable.

Knowledgeable and Friendly Staff

Train your staff to be knowledgeable about various genres, authors, and book recommendations. Encourage them to engage with customers, provide personalized recommendations, and share their own reading experiences. Friendly and helpful staff can enhance the overall customer experience and build long-lasting relationships. When customers feel valued and understood, they are more likely to return.

Ambiance and Background Music

The ambiance of your bookstore should be carefully curated to create an inviting and cozy atmosphere. Consider playing soft background music that complements the bookstore's theme and genre. The right music can set the mood and make your store a place where people want to linger.

Coffee Shop or Reading Corner

Consider incorporating a coffee shop or reading corner within your bookstore. This provides customers with an additional space to relax, socialize, and enjoy their favorite books with a beverage or snack. It adds an extra layer of comfort and convenience, making your bookstore a destination rather than just a retail space.

Customer Service Excellence

Exceptional customer service is vital for the success of any bookstore. It not only helps build customer loyalty but also encourages word-of-mouth marketing. Here are some strategies for providing exceptional customer service:

Personalized Recommendations

Train your staff to actively listen to customers' preferences and offer personalized book recommendations based on their interests. Understanding customers' reading habits and preferences can create a sense of connection and enhance their overall experience. When a customer feels like you've truly understood their tastes, it makes their visit special.

Author Events and Book Clubs

Organize author events, book signings, and book clubs to engage customers and create a sense of community. These events allow customers to connect with their favorite authors and fellow book enthusiasts, providing a unique and memorable experience. Being part of a community of readers can be a powerful draw for your bookstore.

Efficient Checkout Process

Streamline the checkout process to ensure a quick and hassle-free experience for customers. Consider implementing a modern point-of-sale (POS) system that allows for easy payment options, including cash, credit cards, and mobile payments. A smooth checkout experience leaves a positive last impression.

Customer Feedback

Encourage customers to provide feedback on their experience, either through comment cards, online reviews, or surveys. Actively listen to their feedback and take appropriate actions to continuously improve the bookstore's service and overall customer experience. Showing that you value their input can build customer loyalty.

Special Orders

Offer a special-order service where customers can request specific books that are not currently stocked. This demonstrates your commitment to meet individual customer needs and goes a long way in building customer loyalty. Going the extra mile to find a book can make a big difference.

Regular Customer Communication

Stay connected with customers through email newsletters, social media, or a loyalty program. Share updates on new arrivals, upcoming events, and exclusive promotions. Regular communication helps build a relationship with customers and reminds them of your bookstore's offerings.

Encouraging Customer Engagement

Encouraging customer engagement enhances their experience and creates a sense of community within your bookstore. Here are some strategies to encourage customer engagement:

Book Clubs and Discussion Groups

Create book clubs or discussion groups where customers can gather and share their thoughts and insights on featured books. This encourages reading, stimulates conversation, and builds a loyal customer base. Being part of a regular book club can turn occasional visitors into frequent patrons.

Author and Literary Events

Host regular author events, book signings, and literary-themed gatherings. These events provide an opportunity for customers to interact with renowned authors, participate in Q&A sessions, and gain insights into the writing and publishing process. Such interactions can be inspiring and memorable.

Book Launch Parties

Organize book launch parties for local authors or hotly anticipated releases. These events generate excitement in the community and draw customers to your store for an exclusive and memorable experience. A book launch can turn a new release into a community celebration.

Workshops and Lectures

Collaborate with local experts, authors, or community organizations to offer workshops, lectures, or literary-themed classes. This provides customers with an opportunity to learn, engage, and expand their knowledge beyond just reading books. Educational events can make your bookstore a hub of intellectual activity.

Interactive Displays and Competitions

Create interactive displays or competitions that encourage customers to participate and interact with the bookstore. For example, have a "book of the month" competition where customers can vote on their favorite book, or set up a photo booth with literary-themed props for customers to take pictures. Engaging customers in fun activities can create lasting memories.

Conclusion

Providing exceptional service and experience goes beyond just selling books. It's about creating a welcoming and engaging environment, establishing personal connections with customers, and fostering a love for reading and literature. Strive to make every customer interaction a memorable one, and your bookstore will thrive as a result. Your commitment to exceptional service will not only build customer loyalty but also turn your bookstore into a beloved community space.

Chapter 9: Managing Operations and Finances

Managing the day-to-day operations and finances of your bookstore is essential for its long-term success. This chapter will explore key aspects of effectively managing your bookstore's operations and maintaining a healthy financial status.

Setting Up Efficient Operations

Efficiency is the cornerstone of running a successful bookstore. Here are some tips to help you streamline your operations:

Inventory Management:

Proper inventory management ensures that you always have the right books in stock. Consider implementing an inventory management system that tracks sales, monitors stock levels, and provides insights into customer preferences. Regularly review your inventory and adjust stock levels based on demand and market trends. This helps you avoid overstocking or running out of popular titles.

Staff Management:

Your staff plays a vital role in providing excellent customer service and keeping operations running smoothly. Hire people who share your passion for books and have knowledge of different genres. Implement effective training programs to keep your staff updated on new releases and industry trends. Encourage teamwork and create a positive work environment that fosters productivity and engagement. Remember, happy employees often lead to happy customers.

Visual Merchandising:

An appealing and organized layout enhances the browsing experience for your customers. Use attractive displays, signage, and bookshelves to showcase books in an engaging manner. Consider arranging books by genre, theme, or popular author to help customers find what they're looking for easily. Regularly refresh your displays to keep your bookstore visually appealing and interesting.

Financial Management

Effective financial management is crucial for the long-term sustainability of your bookstore business. Here are some important considerations:

Budgeting:

Develop a comprehensive budget that outlines your projected revenue and expenses. Include costs such as rent, inventory purchases, utilities, salaries, and marketing expenses. Regularly review your budget and make adjustments as needed to stay on track. This proactive approach helps you avoid financial surprises and ensures you have the funds necessary to keep your business running smoothly.

Profit Margin Analysis:

Track your profit margins for different book categories or genres to identify which ones generate the highest returns. This information can help you make informed decisions about stocking and pricing strategies. For example, if you notice that a particular genre has a higher profit margin, you might choose to expand your selection in that area.

Pricing Strategy:

Set competitive prices for your books while considering factors such as market demand, competition, and your profit margins. Regularly review your pricing strategy to ensure it aligns with market trends and customer expectations. A well-thought-out pricing strategy can help you attract customers and increase sales.

Cash Flow Management:

Monitor and manage your cash flow effectively to ensure you have enough funds to cover operational expenses. Maintain clear visibility into your accounts receivable and accounts payable to prevent any cash flow gaps. This involves keeping a close eye on when payments are due and ensuring you have sufficient cash on hand to meet your obligations.

Financial Tracking and Reporting:

Invest in accounting software or work with an accountant to accurately track your financial transactions and generate regular reports. These reports will provide insights into your bookstore's financial performance and help you make informed business decisions. Regular financial tracking helps you stay on top of your financial health and quickly identify any issues that need addressing.

Tax Compliance:

Ensure that you meet all legal and regulatory requirements related to tax compliance. Consult with a tax professional or accountant to understand your tax obligations and take advantage of any applicable deductions or credits for your bookstore business. Staying compliant with tax laws helps you avoid penalties and ensures your business operates within legal guidelines.

By implementing efficient operational practices and staying on top of your financial management, you will be able to provide exceptional service to your customers while ensuring the sustainability and growth of your bookstore. In the next chapter, we will delve into providing exceptional customer service and creating a memorable experience for your customers, which is crucial for building a loyal customer base.

Chapter 10: Growing Your Bookstore Business

Growing your bookstore business is essential for long-term success and staying ahead in a competitive market. By implementing effective growth strategies, you can expand your customer base, increase sales, and establish a strong presence in the industry. This chapter will explore various strategies and tactics to help you successfully grow your bookstore business.

Diversify Your Product Offerings

One way to attract new customers and increase sales is by diversifying your product offerings. While books should always remain the core focus of your store, consider expanding into related products and services. For example, you could introduce a section for stationery and journals, book-related merchandise like bookmarks and tote bags, or even offer book-related workshops or events. By providing a wider range of offerings, you can attract a diverse group of customers and encourage repeat visits.

Leverage Online Platforms

In today's digital age, having an online presence is crucial for the growth of any business. Create a user-friendly website that showcases your book inventory, allows customers to make online purchases, and provides information about upcoming events and promotions. Additionally, consider selling your books on popular online platforms such as Amazon or partnering with e-book distributors to cater to readers who prefer digital formats. Embracing online platforms will expand your reach beyond your physical store and attract customers from different locations.

Collaborate with Local Authors and Publishers

Building strong relationships with local authors and publishers can be mutually beneficial. Host book signings or author events to promote their work and drive foot traffic to your store. Offer shelf space for local authors to display their books prominently. By supporting local talent, you not only contribute to the literary community but also create a loyal customer base that appreciates your support for local authors.

Engage with the Community

Participating in community events and initiatives is an excellent way to increase visibility and connect with potential customers. Consider sponsoring local book clubs, partnering with libraries or schools for literary events, or hosting book drives for charitable causes. By actively engaging with the community, you position your bookstore as a trusted and valued member of the neighborhood, which can lead to increased loyalty and support from the local community.

Expand Your Sales Channels

In addition to your physical store, explore other sales channels to increase your reach. Consider setting up pop-up shops at local events or markets, collaborating with coffee shops or cafes to have a small selection of books available for purchase, or even partnering with other local businesses for cross-promotions. By expanding your sales channels, you can reach customers who may not typically visit a bookstore, thereby increasing your customer base and sales opportunities.

Implement Loyalty Programs

Implementing a loyalty program can encourage repeat purchases and increase customer retention. Offer incentives such as discounts, exclusive promotions, or personalized recommendations to customers who join your loyalty program. By rewarding customers for their loyalty, you not only encourage them to continue shopping at your store but also create a sense of belonging and exclusivity.

Continuously Monitor and Adapt

As your bookstore business grows, it's important to continuously monitor market trends, customer preferences, and competition. Regularly assess the performance of your growth strategies and make necessary adjustments. Stay updated on industry news and adapt your offerings and marketing strategies accordingly. By staying proactive and responsive, you can ensure the continued growth and success of your bookstore business.

Conclusion

Growing your bookstore business requires strategic planning, innovation, and staying in tune with market trends. By diversifying your offerings, leveraging online platforms, collaborating with local authors, engaging with the community, expanding sales channels, implementing loyalty programs, and continuously monitoring and adapting, you can position your bookstore for long-term success and become a thriving hub for book lovers.